STATIONS

❖❖❖❖❖❖❖❖❖❖❖❖❖❖❖❖❖❖❖❖❖❖❖❖❖❖❖❖

PLACES FOR PILGRIMS TO PRAY

SIMON BAILEY

SHEFFIELD
CAIRNS PUBLICATIONS
1991

First published 1991

Further copies of this book are obtainable from
Cairns Publications
47 Firth Park Avenue, Sheffield S5 6HF

*Printed by J. W. Northend Ltd
Clyde Road, Sheffield S8 0TZ*

CONTENTS

For my mother

PREFACE

THIS is not a book about railways.
'Stations' are places to stop and wait and think –
places to watch and pray.

Many churches have 'stations of the cross',
the fourteen places to stop and reflect and pray
with Jesus on his last journey,
the journey to the cross.

The stations of this book
are meant to be shared with Jesus too.
You are invited to stop and pray
in places familiar for prayer,
but also in new places,
in unexpected stations.

Then perhaps you will be able
to find your own stations.
They will be places where you alone
stop and wait and think,
where you alone can pray.

"Stay with me, keep watch with me, watch and pray."
[Jesus]

The pattern is the same at every station:
first the place,
then a prayer,
then some words to think about,
then someone to pray for.

FOREWORD

IF getting to God is what life is all about, the way there is rarely easy, and so we need all the help we can get. Making special journeys, pilgrimages to churches or the shrines of saints is something which men and women, boys and girls, have done through the centuries and in every religion and culture. It goes on still. Remember what happened after the dreadful tragedy at Hillsborough football ground?

Christians often like to set up corners in their rooms, perhaps with a picture, a crucifix, a candle, and some flowers. Simple aids to prayer. You don't have to go on a journey to the shrines of Cuthbert or Bede or Julian. Go to your local church or chapel, or go for a walk round the neighbourhood where you live, or stay at home in the quiet of your room, and pray.

This book will help you. It is meant as a guide, but only as a guide. Don't worry if you find yourself praying something else. The author will be delighted, for he knows how important it is to pray, and he wrote this book to help others to pray – but in their own way, which may not be his.

Brother Kenneth
Community of the Glorious Ascension
Telford, January 1990

I
EIGHTEEN STATIONS
in any church, chapel, or cathedral

YOU can look at churches as pieces of history
or you can pray in them.
This is a way of doing both at once.

Before you begin
be quiet for a moment
and say this ancient Irish prayer:

"My respects to you, Jesus Christ;
my respects to you, glorious Virgin;
my respects to you, church of God;
my respects to you, chapel of the Trinity."

Be slow and quiet and take time to pray.

The words to think about all come from the Bible.

1. THE PORCH

STAND in the porch of the church.
In the past the porch was used
for parts of the services.
It is the crossing place,
the threshold,
between the world outside
and a place of sanctuary.

Say:
Living God,
living and strong,
loving and gentle,
pour mercy upon us.

Think about these words:
"I am the Way In.
You will be safe for ever,
enfolded in me."

[*Jesus*]

Pray for
all who come in and go out;
all who look for a way into prayer.

2. THE DOOR

OPEN the door of the church
and stand in the doorway.
Doors do more than keep out draughts:
they mark borders and divisions;
they separate a special place;
they shut us in – or out;
they are to be knocked on, kept open, guarded.
They were also used for centuries
as common noticeboards.

Say:
Living God,
living and strong,
loving and gentle,
pour mercy upon us.

Think about these words:
"Listen carefully
and you will hear me knocking
at the door of your heart.
If you will open the door
I will come in with you
and share your life."

[*Jesus*]

Pray for
those for whom the door seems firmly closed.

3

3. THE FONT

STAND by the font.
Here we become part of the Church.
We are taken into the life of Christ
through the water.
Imagine the font brimming with water.
('Font' comes from the same word as 'fountain'.)
Think of all that water does:
cleans, washes, quenches thirst and flame,
irrigates – and floods,
has power to drown.

Say:
Living God,
living and strong,
loving and gentle,
pour mercy upon us.

Think about these words:
"The old world has been washed off you completely;
you have been set apart for the new."

[*Saint Paul*]

Pray for
all who have been baptized here;
your godparents;
those who search for God in other ways.

4. A SPACE

STAND still in any wide, empty space in the church.
Churches used not to have seats for the people,
and so there was then a great sense of space.
You may be alone here,
but a space like this is always echoing
with the thoughts and prayers and songs
of the thousands who have been here before you.
Add your voice to theirs.

Say:
Living God,
living and strong,
loving and gentle,
pour mercy upon us.

Think about these words:
"All that ever was made I could hear,
in skies and seas and earth,
everything in and beyond was singing:
'Glory to the One who presides as Maker of all
and to the One like a lamb that was given for us.
Let songs of blessing and beauty be sung,
of gentle strength and shining glory,
through ages that never shall end!'"
[*The Seer of Revelation*]

Pray for
space for the song of the earth to be heard;
people whose lives are cluttered.

5. THE NAVE

STAND in the largest part of the church,
take in the size and shape,
the height, the length, the width.
Let it help you to pray.
The word 'nave' comes from the Latin word for 'ship'.
The church is a ship sailing towards God,
out there, beyond us,
and through God, like the sea,
all around us.
Here the people worship;
this is the place for weddings and funerals
and other special events.
In the past a lot of business was conducted here:
people shared every part of their lives with God.

Say:
Living God,
living and strong,
loving and gentle,
pour mercy upon us.

Think about these words:
"You fill the universe and beyond it
even to overflowing.
How much more do you saturate
this little place that we have made!"
[*King Solomon*]

Pray for
all who marry here;
those whose funerals happen here;
those who take care of this church.

6. A WINDOW

STAND by a window.
It may well have stained glass.
It may be very big and full of pictures,
of Jesus or of saints.
It may be plain and small.
Windows let light in,
but the word 'window' comes from Old English
and was originally 'wind eye',
where the wind blew in –
since they had no glass.
Notice the light –
stand in it;
look for the shadows it makes in the church.

Say:
Living God,
living and strong,
loving and gentle,
pour mercy upon us.

Think about these words:
"God is a radiant shining
that is without any shadow of night."
                                    [*Saint John*]

Pray for
all who search for light
   in the midst of dark and miserable places;
the wind of Spirit to blow in every corner.

7. AN ARCH

STAND under an archway.
Notice the particular shape of the arch,
round or pointed, high or low,
heavy or fine and light.
Let the upward curve of the stones
lift you into prayer.

Say:
Living God,
living and strong,
loving and gentle,
pour mercy upon us.

Think about these words:
"The presence of God has come to embrace me here,
this is an entrance to the world of God's Love."
[*Jacob after his dream*]

Pray for
those who find it hard to pray;
those who help others pray.

8. THE ORGAN

STAND where music is made in the church.
There may be choir stalls
or space for other instruments.
Music has been used in churches from the beginning:
Jesus sang a hymn before he went to Gethsemane.
Hymns as we know them have been sung
during the last two or three hundred years.
Before that churches were filled
with the plainsong of the monks.
In this way, using voice and other musical skill,
men and women have used all their gifts
in celebration and worship – and they still do.

Say:
Living God,
living and strong,
loving and gentle,
pour mercy upon us.

Think about these words:
"Overflow with Spirit until together you pour out
the music and melodies of Spirit,
opening your singing hearts to God."
                    [*The writer to the church at Ephesus*]

Pray for
all who make music;
all artists;
the chance to use your own gifts.

9. THE PULPIT AND LECTERN

STAND by the pulpit or lectern.
Both words come from Latin,
pulpit from the word meaning a 'platform',
lectern from the word meaning 'to read'.
The Bible is the collection of books
which holds for us the world of Jesus,
his religion, his followers,
his own teaching and life.
From lectern and pulpit
we hear again the story of hope.

Say:
Living God,
living and strong,
loving and gentle,
pour mercy upon us.

Think about these words:
"I long for the voices of God
more than I could ever long for gold,
much more than even the richest gold.
They melt in the mind like honey,
richer and smoother than the sweetest honey."
[*The psalmist*]

Pray for
all who try to speak for Jesus now;
all writers.

10. THE ALTAR

STAND in front of the altar or holy table.
At the centre of the church is the table
where we share with Jeus his last meal,
his giving of himself for the world.
Here we also glimpse the banquet
there will be for everyone
when that new world of God finally arrives,
the world for which Jesus longed.
We call the table an 'altar'
because here the 'sacrifice' of Jesus
is real again for us.
Here is his life among us too.

Say:
Living God,
living and strong,
loving and gentle,
pour mercy upon us.

Think about these words:
"When you feast on this bread
and share the cup together
you are openly celebrating the death
of Jesus Christ."

[*Saint Paul*]

Pray for
those who minister here;
the coming of God's new world.

11. A DARK CORNER

STAND in the darkest corner you can find.
Churches are often full of dark places
and unexpected corners.
Let them remind you of the mystery we seek,
of the secrecy of prayer,
of the hidden presence of God.

Say:
Living God,
living and strong,
loving and gentle,
pour mercy upon us.

Think about these words:
"When your heart moves you to pray,
choose a place of your own alone,
close the door,
and then open your heart to your Father
who will come to hide with you
in that secret place."

[*Jesus*]

Pray for
people caught in the public eye without escape;
all pilgrims waiting in secret for God.

12. BEHIND THE CURTAIN

STAND where the church clutter is kept.
Every church has a place,
behind a curtain, at the back of the organ,
in the vestry, under the stairs,
where the clutter gathers:
vases, brushes, chairs, dusters.
Here we remember the day to day care of a loved place,
the work behind the clean spaces,
the bright brasses, the polished wood.
Here also is a different memory of the past:
old hymn books, used service sheets,
forgotten robes, some mildew, some neglect.
A church is a human and a changing place too.

Say:
Living God,
living and strong,
loving and gentle,
pour mercy upon us.

Think about these words:
"The clear message of God took root
in the heart of human life,
and set up home in our world
at its most ordinary."

[*Saint John*]

Pray for
those who look after this place;
the mixing of prayer and ordinary life.

13. A BOX FOR GIFTS

STAND near a box or plate
for gifts to people in need.
The Church is all about serving 'the poor':
those in any kind of poverty –
the sick, the lonely, the hungry,
the frightened, the sad, the depressed . . .
in this country and all over the world.

Say:
Living God,
living and strong,
loving and gentle,
pour mercy upon us.

Think about these words:
"If you reach out to do anything
for those who are in need,
you help my own friends –
however low they may have sunk.
And what you have done for them,
you will have done to me as well."
[*Jesus*]

Pray for
a more just world;
people in need.

14. A PRAYER BOARD

STAND by a board or book
where people can write down their own prayers.
The Church offers all the longings,
hopes and needs of the world to God.
These prayers represent that vast and deep range
of human desires and yearnings,
special, private, and unique,
reaching up to God.

Write your own prayer.

Say:
Living God,
living and strong,
loving and gentle,
pour mercy upon us.

Think about these words:
"Give yourselves up to the longing of prayer,
reaching out for God,
praying with a spirit
that is stirred by the Spirit of God."
          [*The writer to the Church at Ephesus*]

Pray for
monks and nuns and others
    who give their lives to prayer;
the praying life of this Church.

15. ANYWHERE – A FAVOURITE PLACE

STAND in the place you like most in the church –
or in any other spot where you know you can pray.
As a focus for prayer some churches keep a little
of the blessed bread and wine from the Holy Communion
in a special place or chapel.
It is usually marked by a candle or light.
Go there.
Or somewhere in the church there may be
a statue or ikon, or a window that moves you,
or a picture or a stone.
Go there.

Say:
Living God,
living and strong,
loving and gentle,
pour mercy upon us.

Think about these words:
"If I let my mind fly on wings
to the sun at the height of the day,
or reach for the deepest fathoms of the sea,
there shall I find your everlasting arms,
even there the sure touch of your gentle hands."
[*The psalmist*]

Pray for yourself.

Say the prayer that Jesus taught us. [p.53]

16. THE CHURCHYARD

IF the church has a place for burials
stand amongst the graves or near a memorial.
The Church is still a focus at death for most people.
Here there is a sense of waiting and of hope,
of rest and of peace,
as well as the sense of mortality,
the death that comes to everyone.

Say:
Living God,
living and strong,
loving and gentle,
pour mercy upon us.

Think about these words:
"We are sighing because of all that has to do with
    death in our lives,
longing for it to be swallowed up by life."
                                              [*Saint Paul*]

Pray for
those you love who have died;
hope and rest and peace.

17. A SPIRE, TOWER, OR CROSS

STAND and look up at the spire or tower of the church –
or the cross at the top.
The building deliberately rises to a climax,
the high point, the cross set over all.
So through the stones and the shape
we are lifted up to everything beyond us –
right in the middle of our lives.

Say:
Living God,
living and strong,
loving and gentle,
pour mercy upon us.

Think about these words:
"I have chosen that above all else
I shall fix my mind on Jesus –
on Jesus fixed with nails to a cross."
[*Saint Paul*]

Pray for
all who try to point beyond the mundane;
all whose lives are marked by the cross.

18. OUTSIDE

STAND outside in the sun or the rain.
Look at the outside of the church.
Look at the surroundings.
Does the church seem to fit in?
The Church is the symbol of other possibilities
in the very middle of our world.

Say:
Living God,
living and strong,
loving and gentle,
pour mercy upon us.

Think about these words:
"In Jesus God stretches out aching arms
to draw the whole world back into love."
                                    [*Saint Paul*]

Pray for
the people who live near this church;
those who try to speak of Jesus in words of today.

II
SEVEN STATIONS
in your home

YOU probably pray at home
as much as you do at church –
or more.
These stations are chosen to help you
watch and pray over your day to day life.
Every home is unique:
you may not have all these separate places,
but adjust the stations for yourself.

Choose a time when the house is empty.
Or use these prayers as part of your routine,
as you happen to be in each place.

The words to think about are the eight verses
of an ancient Celtic prayer-poem about the home.
It is a prayer for protection
and may be used as a 'Caim':
As you say the words you raise your arm,
and, pointing, you draw a circle sun-wise
around yourself in the name of God to protect you.
The circle goes with you as you go.

Begin the Caim:
"O God, bless the place where I live;
give blessing to all that it holds."

Be slow and quiet and take time to pray.

A CAIM

O God bless the place where I live;
give blessing to all that it holds.

O God bless the journeys I make;
give blessing to travel and rest.

O God bless the words that I speak;
give blessing to silence and talk.

O God shield my heart from guilt;
fill our bodies and spirits with joy.

O God bless the folk I live with;
give blessing to your livelihood.

O God let my spirit rise up;
let the darknesses in us go down.

O God shield my heart from distress;
give protection from evil and wrong.

And O God bless my body
To be close to my soul,
So I enter whole into life
With the dear Child of Mary.

1. THE DOOR

GOING through the door –

Leave it open,
and think about the threshold,
the edge between the world outside and home,
your place of security and belonging.
There may be tensions here,
but inside the door you belong.

Say:
Living God,
living and strong,
loving and gentle,
pour mercy upon us.

Think about these words:
"O God bless the journeys I make;
give blessing to travel and rest."

Pray for
each one who comes and goes through your door;
those who sleep in doorways, shut out from a home.

2. THE LIVING ROOM

Go into the main living area, the living room –

Sit down.
This is the base of your life.
This is where you live out your human existence,
living and crying, listening and singing,
talking, thinking, arguing, planning...

Say:
Living God,
living and strong,
loving and gentle,
pour mercy upon us.

Think about these words:
"O God bless the words that I speak;
give blessing to silence and talk."

Pray for
those who share your life;
the lonely.

3. THE KITCHEN

Go into the place where you cook, the kitchen.

Stand by the cooker, the fridge,
or the washing machine.
Perhaps put the kettle on...
Life goes on here too,
but in a slightly different way –
preparation, cleaning up, work,
washing, ironing, storing,
and, again, talking, thinking, planning –
a busy place for many people,
an easy place to wait and pray,
while the hands are busy with other things.

Say:
Living God,
living and strong,
loving and gentle,
pour mercy upon us.

Think about these words:
"O God shield my heart from guilt;
fill our bodies and spirits with joy."

Pray for
all who work here and the care they take;
the arrogant and proud who never serve
    and are afraid to care.

4. THE DINING ROOM

Go into the place where you eat, the dining room.

Sit down where you normally eat meals.
Meals are more than sustenance:
they are human celebration, feast and joy,
friendship and sharing,
welcome for strangers
and the bonding of friends.

Say:
Living God,
living and strong,
loving and gentle,
pour mercy upon us.

Think about these words:
"O God bless the folk I live with;
give blessing to our livelihood."

Pray for
the chance to share more;
the hungry and the poor.

5. THE STAIRS

Go through to the stairs.

Sit at the top of the stairs or in a passage.
Like the door this is another in-between place,
a place for movement and connection.
Why else do so many people like sitting on the stairs
to think and be quiet?
Stairs – going up – hint at hope,
reaching, effort, risk, aspiration.

Say:
Living God,
living and strong,
loving and gentle,
pour mercy upon us.

Think about these words:
"O God let my spirit rise up;
let the darknesses in us go down."

Pray for
all the hopes of your household;
time to watch and think and reach up;
the hopeless and defeated.

6. THE BATHROOM

Go into the place where you wash, the bathroom.

Fill the sink.
Splash the water on your face...
This is the place of refreshment and cleansing,
restoring freshness.
Like that first splash of cold water in the morning...
Bathing and washing are full of echoes
of inner cleansing and renewal.

Say:
Living God,
living and strong,
loving and gentle,
pour mercy upon us.

Think about these words:
"O God shield my heart from distress;
give protection from evil and wrong."

Pray for
a refreshed and renewed spirit
    for all who use this room;
those who feel guilty and dirty,
    stale and corrupt.

7. THE BEDROOM

Go into the place where you sleep, the bedroom.

Lie down on the bed...
This is the place for sleep and rest,
for the ending of the day.
For many it is a place of love too.
For some it is a place of sickness.
It is a very personal place,
a place of dreams,
of long thought into the early hours,
of tears and pain,
private possessions and treasures.
With the thought of sleep
there is always the near or distant echo
of death and final rest.

Say:
Living God,
living and strong,
loving and gentle,
pour mercy upon us.

Think about these words:
"And O God bless my body
To be close to my soul,
So I enter whole into life
With the dear Child of Mary."

Pray for
rest, a quiet mind, a good death;
the bed-ridden, the restless, the loveless.

Repeat the Caim
and this time pray for protection
for all those,
all over the world,
who have no home at all.

Say the prayer which Jesus taught us [p.53]

III
TWELVE STATIONS
in any town, city, or village

THESE stations take you into prayer
in the place where you live –
town, city, village –
so that it becomes a place of pilgrimage.

Say this ancient Celtic prayer before you begin.
It used to be said, under the breath,
for any journey,
short or long, important or not.

"Bless to me, O God,
the earth beneath my feet;
bless to me, O God,
the path whereon I go."

This is secret prayer, not a public display.
Quietly you offer to God the place where you live.
Be slow and quiet and take time to pray.

"Prayer could be silent,
a way of being in the world,
an inward and outward bearing,
a constant striving for increased awareness of the world,
and for the active love, ever renewed,
which must accompany this striving."

[*Petru Dumitriu*]

The words to think about in this part
come from a wide variety of writers and poets,
from different places and times.

1. THE ROAD

Pause
on the road into your town.

Notice
the travellers –
shoppers, workers, school children,
people meeting friends, people talking,
people waiting, people relaxing...

Think
of the beginnings of their journeys –
and of the end.

Question:
Where are you going?

Say:
Living God,
living and strong,
loving and gentle,
pour mercy upon us.

Think about these words:
"While I thought I was climbing
I found myself descending,
having lost my way.
Let me go up and down:
I have no other work to do."
     [*From an early Christian hymn*]

Give thanks
for the journey.

Pray
for all travellers,
for all wayfarers.

2. A SHOP

Pause
in a shop (or outside it):
a supermarket, a corner shop, a chemist,
a florist, a greengrocer...

Notice
the goods, the presentation, the prices,
the shoppers, the workers...

Think
of the needs supplied,
the needs not supplied,
(the excess, the waste...),
of the things you can't buy here.

Question:
What do you really want?

Say:
Living God,
living and strong,
loving and gentle,
pour mercy upon us.

Think about these words:
"The perfect world is pure gift,
and costs everything."
                    [*Don Cupitt*]

Give thanks
for sustenance.

Pray
for more evenly shared resources,
for a sense of proportion.

3. A PUB

Pause
at a pub,
or any place of leisure –
cinema, disco, sports' stadium...

Notice
the faces,
the smiles, the talk, the silences...

Think
of the pleasures shared,
the celebrations of life,
the discomfort and the irritation too.

Question:
What gives you the greatest pleasure?

Say:
Living God,
living and strong,
loving and gentle,
pour mercy upon us.

Think about these words:
".... who kisses a joy as it flies
Lives in eternity's sunrise."
[*William Blake*]

Give thanks
for pleasure.

Pray
for alcoholics.

4. THE TOWN HALL

Pause
at the town hall
or a place representative of government.

Notice
the announcements, notices, leaflets,
the officials, the visitors.

Think
of the order and organization,
the complex system of law, structure, institution,
the efficiency and ordering of human community,
the facelessness and the lack of humanity.

Question:
How do you turn your prayer into politics?

Say:
Living God,
living and strong,
loving and gentle,
pour mercy upon us.

Think about these words:
"Everything important begins in mysticism
and ends in politics."

[*Charles Péguy*]

Give thanks
for an ordered society.

Pray
for the victims of the system.

5. A PARK

Pause
in a park,
in a green place, by a tree.

Notice
how nature fits into your community:
Does it blend or jar?
Do they grow together?

Think
of the place before human beings lived here
(not so long ago . . .),
of the countryside beyond your place,
of the sky above, and the air around.

Question:
What does nature give you?

Say:
Living God,
living and strong,
loving and gentle,
pour mercy upon us.

Think about these words:
"Lift the stone and you will find me,
cleave the wood and I am there."
[*A saying possibly by Jesus*]

Give thanks
for the earth.

Pray
for greater friendship with the earth.

6. A SCHOOL

Pause
by a school
or by any place of learning.

Notice
the building, the people,
its place in the community.

Think
of the learning that goes on,
and the learning that never stops,
that never starts,
the learning that happens elsewhere,
the openness of children.

Question:
How lively is the child in you?

Say:
Living God,
living and strong,
loving and gentle,
pour mercy upon us.

Think about these words:
"Poor-boy – leaves
moon-viewing
for rice-grinding."
   [*Basho, a Zen poet*]

Give thanks
for your own childhood.

Pray
for grace always to go on learning.

7. A CHURCH

Pause
at a church.
Go in if you can.

Notice
how it fits in –
its architecture, age,
height and proportions,
its beauties,
its place in the community now.

Think
of all that has happened here –
all the life events, all the people,
all the longings and the prayers,
all the joy, all the best gifts given.

Question:
What do you find beautiful here?

Say:
Living God,
living and strong,
loving and gentle,
pour mercy upon us.

Think about these words:
"Beauty will save the world."
                    [*Dostoevsky*]

Give thanks
for the worldwide Church.

Pray
for the beauty of its life now.

8. A HOSPITAL OR HEALTH CENTRE

Pause
at the local place for health services.

Notice
the people –
carers and cared for,
the variety of ailments,
the mothers, the dependent, the old...

Think
of all the physically and mentally ill people
in your community;
those frightened of the health system –
the waiting, the drugs, the pain.

Question:
Where are your own wounds?

Say:
Living God,
living and strong,
loving and gentle,
pour mercy upon us.

Think about these words:
"But to our wounds God's wounds alone can speak,
And not a God has wounds, but Thou alone."
                                    [*Edward Shillito*]

Give thanks
for the measure of health you have.

Pray
for the sick and the dying.

9. THE GUTTER

Pause
in the gutter of the road.

Notice
the litter,
the drains...

Think
of the hidden edges of your community –
criminals, prisoners,
the mad, the victims...

Question:
Who have you turned into a victim?
Who have you helped to release?

Say:
Living God,
living and strong,
loving and gentle,
pour mercy upon us.

Think about these words:
"He also said: 'God sells righteousness
at a very low price for those who wish to buy it:
a little piece of bread,
a cloak of no value,
a cup of cold water,
a mite.'"

[*Bishop Epiphanius of Cyprus*]

Give thanks
for carers.

Pray
for all victims.

10. A TELEPHONE BOX

Pause
at a telephone box.

Notice
the machinery
and the people using it.

Think
of all the communications made,
the emergencies,
the arguments and misunderstandings,
the new meetings and the good news.

Question:
In an 'age of communication'
what are you communicating?

Say:
Living God,
living and strong,
loving and gentle,
pour mercy upon us.

Think about these words:
"A long work of nature it was
to smooth and polish all the pebbles of this bay.
A long work it will be,
a labour of mutual abrasiveness,
before in others' company we may sit at ease."
[*Stomar of Fintry*]

Give thanks
for all human contact.

Pray
for the lonely.

11. A FACTORY

Pause
at a factory
or any place of work.

Notice the work done
the products, the people, the place.

Think of the effort and energy used here,
body and mind,
the satisfaction of creating,
the drudgery.

Question:
When was the last time you made something new?

Say:
Living God,
living and strong,
loving and gentle,
pour mercy upon us.

Think about these words:
"To pray is to work:
to work is to pray."
[*An old Latin proverb*]

Give thanks
for all creative work.

Pray
for the unemployed.

12. A STATION

Pause
at a bus station
or a railway station.

Notice
the people waiting –
patient, expectant, restless, lost,
the destinations served...

Think
of the different places
linked together here,
the lives that touch and overlap here,
the journeys ended and begun.

Question:
What are you waiting for?

Say:
Living God,
living and strong,
loving and gentle,
pour mercy upon us.

Think about these words:
"The best journey to make is inward."
[*R. S. Thomas*]

Give thanks
for journeys done.

Pray
for the way ahead.

Say the prayer which Jesus taught us [p.53]

IV
SEVEN STATIONS
around your body

THESE stations are the most personal of all.
Relax, breathe slowly, take off your shoes.
Rest before you begin.
Perhaps listen to some music.

"In this poor body,
composed of one hundred bones
and nine openings,
is something called spirit,
a flimsy curtain swept this way and that
by the slightest breeze."

[*Basho, a Zen poet*]

The words to think about are all translated
from the words of Jesus, recorded in the Gospels.

An old Celtic tale recalls a renowned leader
who was asked the secret of gentleness:
"There is no secret – only –
Christ is always in my heart
and I am always at his feet."

Be slow and quiet and take time to pray.

Sometimes you can use these stations
as a way of praying for someone special to you,
making the journey on that person's behalf.

1. YOUR EARS

BEGIN at your ears.
Touch them.
Listen carefully to every sound.
Simply take in every noise around you.
Listen to the sounds of your own body.
Think of the sounds that disturb you:
screaming, explosions,
loud machinery, angry shouts...
Think of the sounds you love best:
water, wind and rain, the sea,
birds, music, voices...

Say:
Living God,
living and strong,
loving and gentle,
pour mercy upon us.

Listen to the sounds within:
the movement of spirit,
inner voices, music, silence...

Think about these words:
"If you have ears to catch the meaning
and not the words alone,
then listen now."

[*Jesus*]

Pray for attentiveness and discernment.

2. YOUR EYES

MOVE on to your eyes.
Close them, open them, touch them.
Look steadily ahead.
Take in everything in your field of vision.
Distinguish each part and see the whole.
Fix your eyes on some object –
your hand, a plant, a photograph,
a picture, a stone...
beautiful, mysterious, puzzling, difficult.
Look lovingly at it:
shape, colour, size, texture;
see it in two dimensions as if you were painting;
see it in three dimensions.
Take it all in.

Say:
Living God,
living and strong,
loving and gentle,
pour mercy upon us.

Look inwards:
Notice your own colour, shape, texture.
Try to put the two visions together.

Think about these words:
"If the eyes are clear,
you will be full of light within."
                    [*Jesus*]

Pray for vision and insight.

3. YOUR MOUTH

MOVE down to your mouth.
Open it. Touch it.
Breathe in and out,
slowly and deeply.
Let your breathing become rhythmic.

Say aloud your own name. Repeat it.
Think of the thousands of words
that pass your lips every day.
And think of the other ways
in which you use your mouth –
eating, kissing, sneering, smiling . . .

Say:
Living God,
living and strong,
loving and gentle,
pour mercy upon us.

Open your mouth and breathe gently
and think of the gap
between what you feel and what you say,
what you think and the words you find to express it,
what you would like people to hear
and what you actually say.
Think of the joy of words that come from the heart.
Think of the joy of silence.

Think about these words:
"The words on your lips
flow out of the fulness of the heart."
                              [*Jesus*]

Pray for judgment and courage.

48

4. YOUR INSIDES

MOVE inside yourself.
Wrap your arms around yourself.
Close your eyes
and wander through the insides of your body:
bones, muscles, nerves, veins, cells;
organs for eating, moving, sex;
the blood system, the feeling system, the waste system,
all working together...
Feel it all at work as you breathe –
silent, smooth, together.

Say:
Living God,
living and strong,
loving and gentle,
pour mercy upon us.

You are alive.
You have been given life.
This is you.
Enjoy your body,
greet every part,
feel the life.

Think about these words:
"Good things are brought out of the heart-store
that is within good people."

[*Jesus*]

Pray for reverence and support.

5. YOUR FEET

MOVE slowly out and down to your feet.
Stand up and stretch – dance perhaps.
Feel your feet supporting you,
giving you balance, movement, purpose.

Say:
Living God,
living and strong,
loving and gentle,
pour mercy upon us.

Think where your feet have taken you today.
Think of the journeys you make with them.
Feet can be ugly and dangerous,
kicking, marching mindlessly, running away.
Try to tread softly, quietly, purposefully,
keeping your balance.

Think about these words:
"If I, your leader and teacher,
have bathed and refreshed your feet,
you should bathe each other's feet as well."

[*Jesus*]

Pray for sensitivity and strength.

6. YOUR HANDS

AND back up again to your hands.
Stretch out your hands, your fingers.
Hands are even more sensitive and useful than feet –
touching, holding, writing,
moving, pointing,
releasing, supporting, pressing...

Say:
Living God,
living and strong,
loving and gentle,
pour mercy upon us.

Pur your hands together
and feel them there.
Acknowledge them.
Touch and be touched.

Think of the people you've held,
the things you've made,
the things you've given,
the hands you've shaken,
all that you've pushed...

Think about these words:
"When you stretch out your hand in love,
do it so gently that even your left
does not know what your right hand is giving."
[Jesus]

Pray for gentleness and generosity.

7. YOUR MIND

LIE down and think of your mind.
The mind is more than the brain.
It is a spiritual place,
binding you together with your body
to make you who you are – a person.
Relax, think slowly,
feel and reflect,
watch yourself thinking.

Say:
Living God,
living and strong,
loving and gentle,
pour mercy upon us.

Our minds are so busy,
so full of things to do,
to keep going, to worry at.
Let the pool become still.
Let the depths become visible.
Let yourself go below the surface.
Stretch down for the deep places.
Be still. Think. Pray.

Think about these words:
"The new world of God is within you."
[Jesus]

Pray for trust and clarity.

Say the prayer that Jesus taught us:

A Version of the Prayer Jesus taught his friends

FATHER and Mother of us all,
you are love through and through,
and we bless You.
Let Your new world come,
let what You long for be always done,
in everyone, everywhere – and in us.
Be near enough to reach our need every day.
Be gentle enough to forgive us
the hurt we have done to You –
as we are gentle and forgive in our turn.
Never let us fall
but draw us away from evil and the dark.
For we know the world that is coming is Yours,
all Yours, in richness and beauty and splendour.
                                        Amen.

SOURCES
AND ACKNOWLEDGMENTS

PREFACE

Matthew 26.36

PART I

Introduction

FORRISTAL, D. (tr.) *'Saltaire' Prayers from the Irish Tradition.*
Columba Press, 1988.

Stations

1. John 10.9	10. I Corinthians 11.26
2. Revelation 3.20	11. Matthew 6.6
3. I Corinthians 6.11	12. John 1.14
4. Revelation 5.13	13. Matthew 25.40
5. I Kings 8.27	14. II Corinthians 5.4
6. I John 1.5	15. I Corinthians 2.2
7. Genesis 28.17	16. Psalm 139.8–9
8. Ephesians 5.19	17. Ephesians 6.18
9. Psalm 19.10	18. II Corinthians 5.19

PART II

CARMICHAEL, Alexander (tr.), *Carmina Gaedelica.* Scottish
Academic Press, Edinburgh, 1971. Paraphrased by the
author.

PART III

Introduction

Carmina Gaedelica, op. cit.
DUMUTRIU, Petru, *Incognito.*

[*Stations*

Stations

1. Quoted in NEWHALL, Beaumont (ed.), *Frederick H. Evans. An Aperture monograph*, 1973, p.66
2. CUPITT, Don, *Jesus and the gospel of God.* Lutterworth, 1979, p.57
3. BLAKE, William, *Eternity,* in *Poems and Prophecies.* Everyman, 1927, p.383
4. PEGUY, Charles
5. From the Oxyrhyncus Papyrus.
6. BASHO, (tr. STRYK, Lucien) *On Love and Barley.* Penguin Classics, 1985, p.41
7. DOSTOEVSKY, Fyodr.
8. SHILLITO, Edward (1972–1948), *Jesus of the Scars*
9. WARD, Benedicta (ed.), *Sayings of the Desert Fathers.* Mowbrays, 1975, p.50
10. JACKSON, Jordan (ed.), *Stomar of Fintry,* from *The Irish Anthology*
11. Anonymous
12. THOMAS, R. S. *Groping,* from *Later Poems.* Macmillan, 1983.

PART IV

Introduction

BASHO, op. cit. p.10
REITH, Martin, *God in our Midst.* SPCK, 1975, p.28

Stations

1. Mark 4.9
2. Matthew 5.22
3. Luke 6.45b
4. Luke 6.45a
5. John 13.14
6. Matthew 6.3
7. Luke 17.21

All verses of Scriptures have been translated and interpreted by the author. Both he and the publisher are grateful to holders of copyright for permission to quote and apologize for any unintended omissions.